let's
Paint

Ivan Bulloch & Diane James

WORLD BOOK / TWO-CAN

Art Director: Ivan Bulloch
Editor: Diane James
Design Assistant: Peter Clayman
IIIustrator: Emily Hare
Photographer: Daniel Pangbourne
Models: Abi, Courtney, Natalia, Shelby, Jonathan,
Grant, Stephanie
Special thanks to: Karen Ingebretsen, World Book Publishing

First published in the United States and Canada in 1997 by
World Book, Inc.
525 W. Monroe
20th Floor
Chicago, IL USA 60661
in association with Two-Can Publishing Ltd.

**For information on other World Book products,
call 1-800-255-1750, x 2238.**

ISBN: 0-7166-5602-7 (hbk)
ISBN: 0-7166-5603-5 (pbk)
LC: 96-61755

Printed in Spain

1 2 3 4 5 6 7 8 9 10 01 00 99 98 97 96

Contents

splish, splash!

You'll be amazed at how many things you can do with a few jars of paint and some brushes. You'll need a few other things too. Some projects are a little messy, so have an apron and some newspaper handy! On a sunny day, you could paint outside!

loads of new ideas to try...have fun!

1 Try these quick, easy ideas to start with. Mix up some paint with a little water. It should be creamy, not too runny. Dip a large brush in the paint and flick it downward over a sheet of paper. Splish, splash – keep going!

2 Next, scrunch up a small piece of newspaper or tissue. Dab the crumpled ball in some creamy paint and make lots of prints on a sheet of paper.

don't shake hands with me!

3 Now paint the palm of your hand with some fairly thick paint. Press down on a sheet of paper and lift your hand off to make a perfect print. Make lots more prints!

turn the page and keep painting...

5

quick print

Make your own print blocks and decorate some plain sheets of paper. When you want to wrap a present for a friend, you will have paper ready! Try all sorts of different papers – from tissue paper to newspaper to plain old brown paper.

sponge and string patterns

1 Choose a simple shape that you like. Draw it on a piece of thin kitchen sponge using an extra-thick marker.

2 Cut out the sponge shape and glue it to a square of cardboard using water-resistant glue. This is your first print block. Now make some different kinds of print blocks!

you'll never guess what's in here!

3 Wind a length of string into a shape you like and glue it to a piece of cardboard. Make another print block by gluing on dry pasta shapes.

4 To make prints, cover one of your print blocks with thick paint. Press the block onto a sheet of colored paper. Lift it off and enjoy your first print. Make lots more!

7

sunny stones

You'll find all sorts of things to do with your painted pebbles and stones. They can stop pieces of paper from blowing away in the wind, keep doors open, help to decorate your room, and even add a bit of fun to your yard.

1 Look for different-sized stones when you go outside. Be careful not to disturb any creatures you might find hiding under them. You can also buy stones from most garden centers.

what's it going to be?

2 Wash your stone first. When it's dry, draw a design on it. Paint the first color and leave it to dry.

which one do you like best?

3 Paint each color in turn, letting your stone dry between coats.
Keep your design as simple as possible.
If you want to put your stones outside, cover them with a coat of clear varnish.

peek-a-boo

Hide behind one of these jolly masks
and nobody will know who you are!
Then pop out from behind
the mask and give your
friends a big surprise!

surprise, surprise!

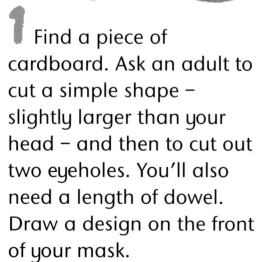

1 Find a piece of
cardboard. Ask an adult to
cut a simple shape –
slightly larger than your
head – and then to cut out
two eyeholes. You'll also
need a length of dowel.
Draw a design on the front
of your mask.

2 Paint your mask in different colors, letting each color dry before starting on the next.

3 Now paint stripes on the dowel. When it's dry, tape the dowel firmly to the back of the mask.

guess who?

frame it!

You've painted the best picture in the world. Now it needs a frame that's just as spectacular! Here's how to make one.

mooooo!

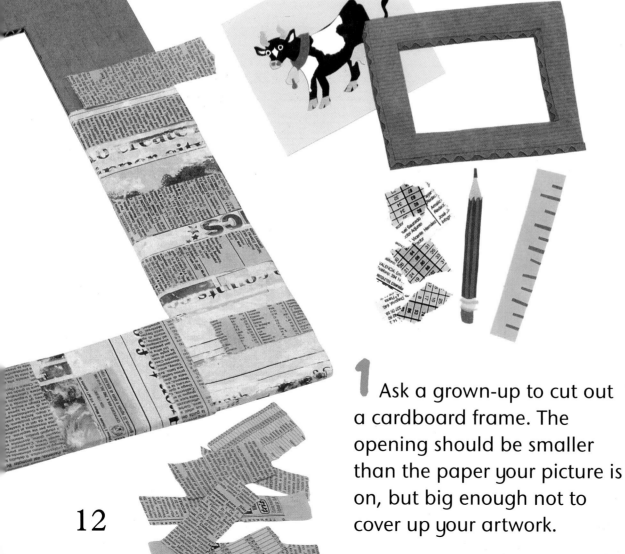

2 Mix some flour and water together to make a creamy paste. Tear a sheet of newspaper into strips.

3 Use the paste to stick the strips of paper all over the frame – back and front. Two or three layers will make a strong frame.

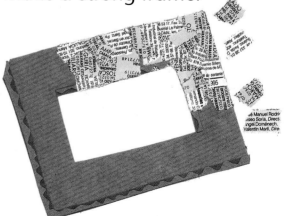

1 Ask a grown-up to cut out a cardboard frame. The opening should be smaller than the paper your picture is on, but big enough not to cover up your artwork.

what a pretty picture!

4 When the newspaper is dry, you can paint your frame. Use one color, or make a pattern with as many colors as you like.

5 Wait for the paint to dry, and then tape your picture to the back of the frame. Make lots of frames and you can put on an art show for all your friends!

pretty pots

The next time you give someone a plant, make it a special surprise by decorating the pot in snazzy colors. Choose a terra cotta pot and start painting. Make one for yourself, too!

2 You may find it easier to paint your pot if you stand it upside down. Paint on the first color, using your marks as a guide.

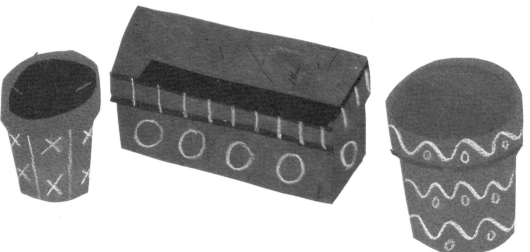

1 Pots come in all sorts of shapes and sizes – long window boxes, small flower pots, and huge urns. Decide on a pattern and draw it on the pot with a piece of chalk. Make it simple!

3 When the paint is dry, add the next color. Use a fairly thick brush to make the painting go more quickly. Protect your pot with a coat of clear varnish.

here's one especially for you!

tiger growls

Don't let animals have all the fun! You can turn yourself into a fierce, growling tiger or another animal in no time.

grrrrr!

1 Cut a large sheet of stiff paper or thin cardboard, big enough to cover the top part of your body. Decide what animal you want to be and paint that animal's background color first.

2 Add spots or stripes using different colors. You could try some of the quick printing ideas from the beginning of the book.

3 Cut a strip of cardboard about 2 inches (4cm) wide. It should be long enough to attach to both sides of your animal body and go around the back of your neck.

4 Glue or tape each end of the strip of cardboard to the top of your animal body. Slip the loop over your head. Decorate your face with special face paints and leap into action.

clever cards

Here's a great trick that will save loads of time if you want to make more than one picture of the same thing! It's called stenciling. Use it to make cards for all your friends!

1 Draw a simple picture on thin cardboard. Cut the shape from the middle of the card. You may need a grown-up to help with this.

cock-a-doodle-doo!

2 Fold a piece of colored paper – larger than your stencil – in half to make a card. Use masking tape to attach the stencil to the front of the card.

18

just a few more dabs!

3 Use a small sponge or a special stencil brush with short, stubby bristles to dab paint into your stencil. Let the paint dry.

4 Undo the tape, lift off your stencil, and you will see your picture! You can use your stencil again and again.

19

building blocks

Build colorful monsters, space stations, and anything else you can think of with your own giant building blocks. Collect as many different containers, tubes, and boxes as you can find, and start painting.

2 Paint your boxes and tubes all over with the first color. You may need to paint them again when the first coat is dry to make a strong, solid color.

1 Gather a collection of old containers. Make sure they are clean and dry. You may need to soak them first, so you can peel off the labels.

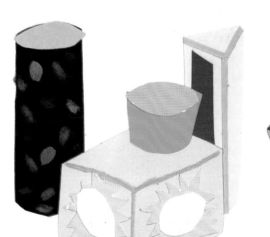

save your old boxes!

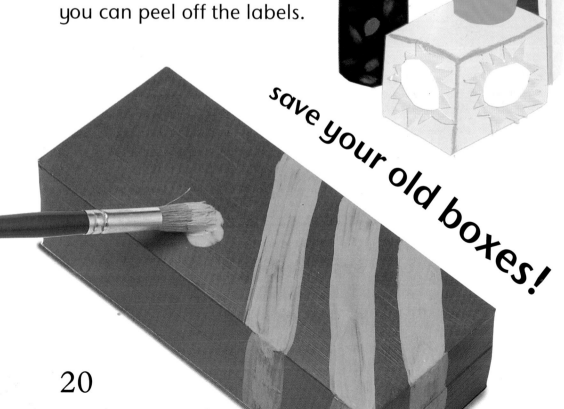

3 Now add another color by painting, sponging, or splattering on a pattern. When the paint is dry, you can start building things with your blocks.

21

wall painting

To make a giant painting, you'll need some friends to help! Use any kind of paper for the background – even old newspaper or brown wrapping paper.

get your paint and brushes out

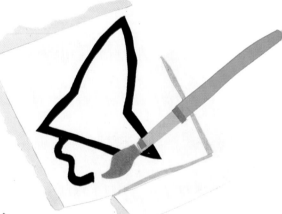

1 Choose a theme for your picture. Get your friends together and paint bold, black outline shapes on plain paper. Or you could use thick markers.

2 Now ask your friends to paint their pictures in bright colors. They can add patterns, too, the more cheerful the better! Let the pictures dry.

3 Cut around the outlines and lay the pictures out. Tape the sheets of paper to the wall and glue on the pictures. Write your friends' names on the pictures.

tips and tricks

Here are some of our favorite tips to help you with your painting.

1 Look for ready-mixed paints in squeezable containers.

2 Paint large areas of color first. Add details when the paint is dry.

3 Cover your work surface with newspaper. This will help keep your work area clean.

4 When you are using glue or varnish, read the instructions on the bottle or tube. They will tell you how to use these substances safely and correctly.

5 Save empty yogurt containers. They will be useful for storing brushes. The lids are good for mixing paints.

6 Take good care of your paintbrushes. Rinse them well and dry them out thoroughly after every use.